Touch

First published in the U.S. in 1994 by Carolrhoda Books, Inc.
c/o The Lerner Group
241 First Avenue North, Minneapolis, Minnesota 55401

Copyright © 1993 Wayland (Publishers) Ltd., Hove, East Sussex
First published 1993 Wayland (Publishers) Ltd.

Library of Congress Cataloging-in-Publication Data

Suhr, Mandy.
    Touch / written by Mandy Suhr ; illustrated by Mike Gordon.
        p.   cm. – (I'm alive)
    Originally published: Wayland Publishers, 1993.
    ISBN 0-87614-837-2
    1. Touch–Juvenile literature. [1. Touch. 2. Senses and
sensation.] I. Gordon, Mike, ill. II. Title. III. Series: Suhr, Mandy.
I'm alive.
QP451.S84 1994   93-44192
612.8′8–dc20   CIP
                                                                  AC

Printed in Italy by Rotolito Lombarda S.p.A., Milan
Bound in the United States of America

1 2 3 4 5 6 – P/OS – 99 98 97 96 95 94

Touch

written by Mandy Suhr
illustrated by Mike Gordon

Carolrhoda Books, Inc.
Minneapolis

Close your eyes.
Touch some things
around you.

4

How many different
kinds of things can
you feel?

Some things feel hard...

and some things feel soft.

Some things
feel smooth...

8

and some things feel rough.

Some things
feel dry…

or wet…

or even slimy!

The way something
feels is called its
texture. Some things
have a different texture
on the outside than
on the inside.

13

You can feel things when you touch them because you have special touch receptors in your skin.

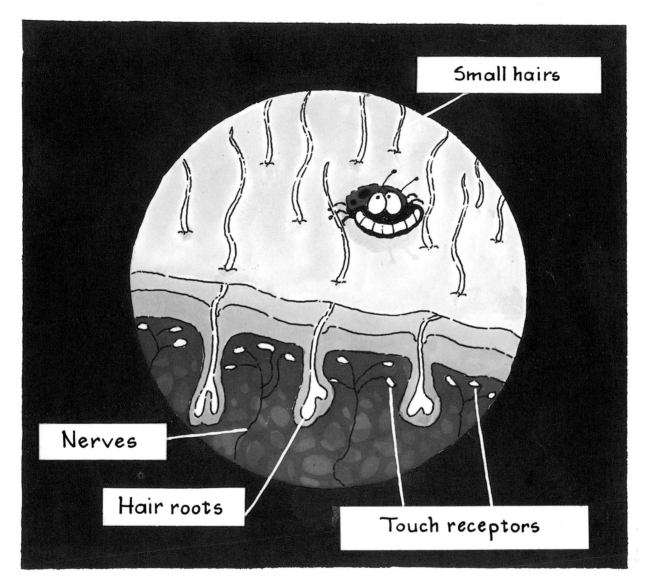

You need a very strong microscope
to see touch receptors.

When you touch something,
nerves carry messages to
your brain.

Then your brain uses these messages
to figure out what you are touching.

Nerves send messages to
your brain if you touch
something that feels
hot or cold.

Your brain reads these messages
and tells you to move if something
is too hot.

Some parts of your body, like your fingers and lips, are better at feeling than other parts. This is because there are more receptors there.

Can you figure
out which parts
are good
at feeling?

Touch is especially useful to people who can't see. They can feel what people look like, even though they can't see them! This is because your brain can use the messages sent by your nerves to figure out what something looks like.

Lizzy can read by touching. She
can't see the special letters.

a b c d e f g

h i j k l m n

o p q r s t u

v w x y z

But she can feel them because they
are raised on the page.

What is your favorite texture?
Can you describe how it feels?

Play this game with a friend.
Make a "feely" box.

28

Can your friend guess what is
in it just by feeling?

A note to adults

"I'm Alive" is a series of books designed especially for preschoolers and beginning readers. These books look at how the human body works and develops. They compare the human body to plants, animals, and objects that are already familiar to children.

Here are some activities that use what kids already know to learn more about their sense of touch.

Activities

1. Take your sense of touch on a walk! Notice the roughness of the bricks on the side of a building, the softness of a flower petal, and the squishiness of mud under your bare feet. Be sure to notice temperature too. How many different textures and temperatures can you find?

2. Make a texture collage. Gather a bunch of things with many different textures. You might use aluminum foil, materials like velvet and corduroy, or bark from a tree. Arrange the things you've gathered on a piece of construction paper and glue them in place. When you display your work, be sure to tell people, "Don't just look–please touch!"

3. Gather a variety of leaves of different sizes and textures. Place the leaves under a thin piece of paper and color over them with the side of a crayon. The leaves will appear on the paper. Notice how the different textures of the leaves show up in your drawing.

4. Take a feather and gently touch different parts of your body. Which is more sensitive, the tip of your nose or your earlobes? Is it easier to feel the feather on the backs of your hands or the bottoms of your feet? The areas that are most sensitive have the most touch receptors.

I'm alive!

Titles in This Series